Explanation of THE RULE OF BENEDICT

BY HILDEGARD OF BINGEN

Translated,
with introduction, notes and commentary,
by Hugh Feiss, osb

PEREGRINA PUBLISHING CO.
Toronto, Ontario

Peregrina Translations Series 15
ISBN 0–920669–15–8
ISSN 083–7092

1995

First published 1990

Printed and bound in Canada

Peregrina Publishing Co.
17 Woodside Avenue
Toronto, Ontario M6P 1L6
416–604–3111

CONTENTS

INTRODUCTION

INTRODUCTION

HILDEGARD AND HER WORKS

The outline of Hildegard's life is well known, thanks to the attention she has received recently from mediævalists.[1] According to the reconstruction of Sr. Marianna Schrader,[2] Hildegard's noble and numerous family came from Bermersheim, near Alzey, about ten miles from Mainz. The family was well connected in church and civil society, although it did not belong to the highest ranks of the nobility. When she was abbess, Hildegard would allow only women of noble family to join the convent at the Rupertsberg, which included members of the highest nobility, such as Richardis von Stade.[3] Later, her brothers gave some of the family property to the convent on the Rupertsberg.

Hildegard was born in 1098, the tenth and youngest child born of her parents, Hildebert and Mechtild.[4] While she was still a small child she had a visionary experience; it was also during childhood that she was troubled by illness.[5] At the age of eight she was sent to the recently refounded Benedictine monastery of Disibodenberg.[6] There she was enclosed with an anchoress named Jutta, the beautiful young daughter of a local count. Soon others attached themselves to Jutta, and her cell expanded to become a convent subject to the abbot of Disibodenberg. In 1136 Jutta died and Hildegard succeeded her as leader of the community. Five years later she had a vision of blinding light when gave her heavenly understanding of the Bible. In the vision she was told to write down what she had seen and heard, but she hesitated to do so for a long time. She became ill and interpreted this as a sign of divine displeasure. So, with the help of the monk Volmar and of Richardis von Stade, she began writing down the visions which underlay her first work, *Scivias* ["scite-vias-domini: know the ways of the Lord"] and which she finished some ten years later.[7] Meanwhile, a commission appointed by Pope Eugene III at Trier in 1147–1148 had approved her visions as authentic.

About this time Hildegard announced that she had a command from God to move her community to Rupertsberg, at the confluence of the Nahe and the Rhine, about fifteen miles from Disibodenberg. With the help of another illness and some outside support, Hildegard and her community of about twenty nuns made the move around 1150. Although there were disputes between the two communities for some years, the community of Disibodenberg did agree to supply a chaplain. To the early years at Rupertsberg probably belong many of Hildegard's hymns and sequences[8] and her medical and scientific works,[9] all of which may have served the liturgical and physical well-being of the new community and its guests.

Meanwhile, Hildegard was becoming more widely known in the world and she corresponded with many important people.[10] Although she was ill between 1158 and 1161, she found the energy to keep working at her second major work, *Liber vitæ meritorum* [Book of Life's Merits].[11] She also went on some preaching tours to monasteries and other churches, which took her considerable distances by river and land. In 1163 she began her *Liber divinorum operum* [Book of Divine Works],[12] which took her over ten years to complete. About 1165 her community made a foundation across the Rhine at Eibingen;[13] in 1170 wrote the *vita* of St. Disibod—but only after she had suffered another bout of sickness—and in 1170/71 she went on another preaching tour.

In about 1174 Volmar, her advisor and confessor, died and his place was taken, temporarily, first by Ludwig from St. Eucharius at Trier and then by Hildegard's nephew, Wezelin from St. Andreas at Cologne. Finally, after Hildegard appealed to the pope, a monk named Godfrey was sent from Disibodenberg around the beginning of 1175. He began writing a life of the abbess but died in 1176 before he could finish it.[14] His secretarial work was taken over by Hildegard's brother Hugo who was replaced as chaplain by a canon of Mainz. Around this same time,the monk Guibert of Gembloux began corresponding with Hildegard.[15] When Hugo and the canon died in 1177, Guibert replaced them both and he remained at Rupertsberg until 1180. During the last year of her life, Hildegard was involved in a dispute with the clergy of Mainz over the burial of a man who had been excommunicated. It was settled before her death on September 17, 1179.

CIRCUMSTANCES OF HILDEGARD'S EXPLANATION OF THE RULE OF BENEDICT

There are several puzzling aspects about this short work of Hildegard. For one thing, although she was a member of a Benedictine convent for all her adult life and an abbess for over forty years, in her works she very seldom mentions Benedict or his *Rule*.[16] This may simply have been another instance of her practice of avoiding quotations from human authorities. In any case, we must rely on this short work for most of what we know of Hildegard's views on monastic practice.[17] Practice, it would seem, is the focus of the work, for Hildegard does not comment on the more theological aspects of Benedict's teaching.

One slight clue to the time of composition may be the preface to the *Liber vitæ meritorum* which mentions that she had been spending time on "answers and admonitions to many persons great and small . . . and letters, with certain other expositions.[18] If her *Explanation of the Rule of St. Benedict* was among these expositions, then she wrote it in the late 1150s or early 1160s.

The identity and location of the recipients of *The Explanation* are even more intractable. The letter requesting the commentary comes from the "congregatio Hunniensis." Scholarly suggestions regarding the identity of this community include the convent of Cluniac nuns at Huy near Liège, Heningense in the diocese of Worms, and Ravengiersburg (Hunsrück) in the diocese of Trier.[19] The petitioners seem to be males ("perjuri" in par. 3), followers of the *Rule of St. Augustine* ("B. Pater Augustinus . . . religionem nostram" in par. 4). Their lack of clarity about observance seems unlikely in such a venerable house as Ravengiersburg, especially since it was surrounded by houses following the carefully elaborated customs of Springiersbach.[20] It seems more likely that a small, out-of-the-way canonical house with eclectic customs drawn from various sources (Chrodegang, Benedictines) was accused by the Benedictines of lax observance. To acquire authority for their existing practices and/or advice on how to reform their customs, they asked Hildegard, a recognised Benedictine authority. Whatever theory one advances, however, it remains difficult to know why Hildegard answered their rather general letter with such a specific reply. Perhaps a messenger brought not just the letter, but some specific questions. In any case, puzzling as the identity of "Hunniensis" is, it does not seem to affect the interpretation of the text very much.

As Pitra noted,[21] Hildegard's style in the *Explanation of the Rule of Benedict* is simpler and more straightforward than elsewhere. Only at the beginning and end is there a hint of her prophetic and visionary experience.

TEXT AND TRANSLATIONS

The letter from the "congregatio Hunniensis cœnobii" and Hildegard's response, the *Regulæ S. Benedicti Explanatio*, are printed among her works in volume 197 of Migne's *Patrologia Latina*, cols. 1053–1066. Migne reprinted the text from volume 23 of the *Maxima bibliotheca veterum patrum* (Lyons, 1677) which, in turn, reprinted the text from J. Blanckwalt, ed., *Epistolarum liber* (Cologne, 1566).[22] None of these printed editions is wholly satisfactory. The text is here translated from Migne (M), but with corrections drawn from the Riesenkodex, Wiesbaden, Hessische Landesbibliothek MS 2 (W)[23] and Pitra (P), Analecta Sacra 8:495. The footnotes to the translation indicate variants in these sources and which reading I have chosen to follow.

Three modern translations offered some guidance in rendering difficult passages: M. Pot's Dutch translation, a German translation and paraphrase by Maria Assumpta Hönmann, "Die Regula Sancti Benedicti (RB) im Kommentar der heiligen Hildegard von Bingen" *Artz und Christ* 27 (1981): 32–45, and a translation prepared by Pamela Jouris as part of an MA thesis at Bishop's University, Lennoxville, Québec, 1990. The divisions and subtitles are my own, although I have profited by the suggestions of Hönmann, as listed on p. 35 of her translation of Hildegard's Explanation.

My commentary follows the paragraph numbers of the translation, The prefix PE refers to the paragraphs of the petitionary letter, while the prefix Ex refers to the paragraphs of Hildegard's *Explanation of the Rule* and my commentary on it.

REQUEST OF THE COMMUNITY OF THE CONVENT OF HUNNIENSIS TO HILDEGARD

1.

To Hildegard, the temple of the Holy Spirit and Christ's revered bride, beloved of God, and to the sisters of the greatly desired mistress of St. Rupert in Bingen.[24] The whole community of the convent of Ravengiersburg, with the humility and insistence of good deeds, [prays] that she be exalted with eternal glory.

2.

As though sprinkled with the priceless flower of the narcissus of paradise,[25] we have so delighted up to now in the revelations of your thought, that we are compelled to say with the apostle: "Thanks be to him who always triumphs in us, in who he displays the fragrance of his knowledge everywhere" (2 Cor 2.14). As we contemplate the whole framework of the entire body of the church in which "the one Spirit divides up to each as he wishes" (1 Cor 12.11), we rejoice that his abundance overflows in your outstanding holiness. Because in post-apostolic time we contemplate you as a mirror of divine love, in a moment of need we flee to you as to the steadfast refuge of an impregnable city, and we entreat you to aid us with your counsel and prayers.

3.

Although we are different from you[26] in all respects, our order is honoured and blessed by you. We have been told of your deeds, how in a short time you bestowed desirable riches on the children of the resplendent church. Because you do not lack this gift now, we cast ourselves[27] at the feet of your holiness and all of us together ask your holy love, that you leave to us as a memorial what is needful to us regarding the *Rule* of our blessed father Benedict.

4.

For we are called liars, perjurers and[28] violators of that aforesaid *Rule*, and people who hold in contempt the synodal decrees. What happens most especially is that if, by the wilfulness of their mind, any of our prelates comes[29] to think contemptuously of the canonical statutes of the *Rule*, then as a law unto themselves they say—according to the testimony of the *Rule* itself—that what they want is holy and just, and what they do not want they think is not allowed (RB 1.9). Hence, it comes to pass that we are carried about by every wind of doctrine (Eph 4: 14) and the presumptions of men weigh[30] heavy on us. Our blessed father Augustine also shuddered at such presumptions. He spoke of them in the same way. He wished our religious community to be free from them, by the grace of God, for a few obvious sacramental celebrations. Although it may not be against faith, they oppress our religious community with servile burdens to such an extent that the state of the Jews would be more bearable. For although they[31] did not know the time of true liberty, they were subject to the sacraments of the law,[32] not to human presumptions.

5.

You would present a work more precious than the riches of Croesus or indeed of all the treasuries of the world, if you would meet our request in this matter of necessity[33] for all cloisters. Even if you were to expound the whole of sacred scripture, you could not present us with anything so useful and so dear. For the rest, pray for us, so that through the Holy Spirit our gathered community may not ever be disturbed by any hostile trickery. But[34] may he who has begun a good work in us (Phil 1:6), deign to preserve it in us by the working of his good will. May your maternal love prosper.

THE RULE OF ST. BENEDICT EXPLAINED BY S. HILDEGARD[35]

INTRODUCTION. THE VIRTUES OF ST. BENEDICT, THE INSPIRED AUTHOR OF THE RULE

1. *Inspiration*

And I, a poor little female in form, unlearned by human teaching, looked toward the true light and to the memory of blessed Benedict as you requested, in order that the matters in the teaching of the *Rule* which are more difficult and obscure to human understanding might be revealed to me through the grace of God. And I heard a voice from the true light saying to me: The Holy Spirit effected most brilliant gifts[36] and mystic inspirations in St. Benedict, so that his mind glowed with the love of God, and by his virtues he shone like the dawn.[37] He performed in his deeds none of the things the crafty devil urged. He had been so filled with the grace of the Holy Spirit that in no deed of his did he lack the power of the Holy Spirit for even a second or the blink of an eye.

2.
Discretion

Furthermore, he was a closed fountain (Song 4:12) who poured forth his doctrine in the discretion of God. For he drove in the sharp nail of his doctrine neither too high nor too low, but in the middle of the wheel, so that each one, whether strong or weak or sick,[38] would be able to drink from his according to his capacity. This turning wheel (cf. Ez 1:15; 10; 9; Dn 7:9) is the power of God, by which God worked in the saints of old up to the time of Moses, who gave the law to the people of God. By the same power God was at work in other holy men as well, the nail of whose labours was fixed at such great height that the common people were not able to grasp it.

3.
Fear, Piety, Charity and Chastity

Blessed Benedict drank his doctrine most mildly in the fear of God; he taught the commandments of God in piety; he constructed the wall of the *Rule*'s holiness in charity; and in chastity he was a stranger to the pomps and delights of this world. Because he wrote his doctrine in fear and piety and in charity and chastity, nothing should be added to or taken away from that doctrine. Nothing is lacking in it because it was done and completed in the Holy Spirit.

4.
Paternal Teacher

Because he was the son of a dove (cf. Mt 3:16–17 par.), he said: "Listen O Son,[39] to the precepts of your father" (RB Prol. 1). Thus, he was full of the holiness of the virtues mentioned above, just as "Moses was the meekest of all the people who lived on the earth" (Nm 12: 3).

A. Searching for God in the Monastic Life

5.
The Kinds of Monks
[RB 1]

As[40] a loving father he says that some monks diverge in their habits of life; to those who ponder this, it is clear how the reward of their deeds will be given them in accord with their merits. For before the time of blessed father Benedict, monks were fortified by no certain rule, and they wandered here and there, uncertain and unstable in various ways. They lacked certain teaching and a fixed place. For this reason he describes the evil elements of their lack of moral stability as a warning that their way of life should be avoided by faithful monks.

6.
On Silence
[RB 6]

On account of the importance of silence, permission to speak[41] is rarely given (cf. RB 6:3) to those who truly are followers of his teaching. Such permission is granted when there arise things requiring consultation or business matters or serious needs; such permission is for speaking together, moderately and briefly as need dictates, not privately.[42] Then when a sign is given, let all be quiet in silence as is customary. Benedict had not predetermined this permission for a stated hour on a certain day, but retained the power to grant it insofar as it was necessary. For he gave this permission to speak[43] only as some just need or kindly purpose urged it. However, since it is almost[44] inhuman for a person to be silent always and never speak, the same father left this matter, as he did many other things, in the power of the judgement of the abbot. He may provide a suitable time for the disciples to speak together about matters which are good and necessary, so that they will not be burdened with weariness because of excessive silence. After such permission to speak together, they could all the more fittingly and sternly be urged and compelled to the spirit and practice of silence.

7. Prayer: The Arrangement of the Divine Office [RB 8–20]

He says: "In the winter, that is from the first of November until Easter, prudent consideration suggests that rising take place at the eighth hour of the night. By resting until a little past midnight, they may rise with digestion complete" (RB 8:1). This is because one who keeps watch for a third part of the night hours in the winter, or who sleeps for a third part of the night and day hours in winter, is not weakened in his brain or in the rest of his body by staying awake or by sleep. Someone who stays awake immoderately, or who sleeps immoderately, suffers damage to his senses and body. Thus the sleeping brothers will[45] rise for vigils with digestion completed because after[46] food has been eaten and drink taken, it is changed[47] into something else during these prolonged hours of inactivity. Then a person should get up, for these vigils also confer health on a person when he shakes himself from his idle sleep and purges himself. If a person sleeps immoderately, he will easily fall victim[48] to fevers and because of the interior heat, he will feel stirring[49] in his flesh. But to guard himself from these things and faithfully serve God, let him with a good attitude fulfil the exhortation of his loving father.

8.

There follows: "Those brothers who need to study the psalter or readings may devote the time after vigils to such meditation" (RB 6:3). He says this to warn them not to give themselves afterwards to sleep or idleness; instead, this winter interlude is carefully arranged for the utility of the soul as the season then permits until, at the dawning of the day, morning praise begins. He assigns this interval after vigils, that is after the nightly psalms are finished, for prayerful meditation or reading. Then immediately he says of the interval in the summer: "From Easter until November 1, the hour for vigils should be arranged that a very small interlude will give the brother a chance to go out for the needs of nature. Then as the day begins to break, lauds are to begin" (RB 6: 4). One should notice in this passage that both in summer and in winter, that is whether there are three readings or only one, the brothers do not return to rest on their beds either after vigils nor after lauds. Rather, in both instances they so arrange the nightly vigils after midnight that they are already singing lauds as they see the day dawn. They will not be burdened by this proper and moderate arrangement. On the contrary, they will rejoice because, to repeat what was mentioned earlier, when a man keeps vigil after he has rested for more than half the night and then is awakened, his strength is not undermined by such vigils.

9.

Then he says: "When these have been recited and a verse said, let the abbot give a blessing" (RB 9:5). This does not indicate that the Lord's Prayer preceded there; the same is true when he writes regarding the first nocturn on Sunday: "As we said above, when six psalms and the verse have been said and all are sitting in orderly fashion on their benches, four other lessons are to be read from the book, as we said above" (RB 11:2). Nor is the Lord's Prayer mentioned in connection with the second and third nocturn, because after the third nocturn is finished, he says: "After the verse has been said and the abbot's blessing, another four lessons are to be read" (RB 11:7). He makes no mention of the Lord's Prayer there so that it will not be an interruption.

10.

But when the six psalms of the second nocturn of an ordinary day are finished, he says: "After these, the reading from the Apostle follows; it is to be recited by heart" (RB 9:10). And after these, "instead of three lessons, one from the Old Testament is to be pronounced from memory" (RB 10.2). And again; "Then one lesson of the Apostle recited by memory" follows (RB 13:11). This shows that while the brothers devote themselves to readings and meditation,[50] they commit to memory the necessary passages in Holy Scripture. Then when the proper time comes and they need to,[51] they can produce these lessons by heart and from memory without any written material, that is they will recite without a book, for these lessons are short. Because of their brevity, it will be no hindrance should they have at hand no book to read or no light to see. But he is silent about these matters in the day hours of the work of God, because during daylight he leaves it to their judgement whether to recite the chapters, that is the lessons mentioned above, either by heart and from memory or from a codex. There will be less hindrance then because of the daylight.

11.

He commands that the Gospel be read after the nocturns on Sunday and other solemnities. He wants it to be understood that at all times, that is both at night and during the day, the message of God should be heard and practised and, in this way, God be served. Furthermore, when the Gospel has been heard, let the monks remember that saying of the Gospel: "Behold we have left everything and followed you" (Mt 19:27). And he also intended[52] that if anyone, because of scarcity of priests or because of the hindrance of some occupation, was not able to have Mass that day or to be present at it, it will be enough that he has read and heard the Gospel.

12.

When the Gospel has been read, he says: "After the benediction has been given," that is by the customary prayer "let them begin lauds" (RB 11:10). This text does not indicate that an interval should be kept[53] for meditative prayer or readings; nor does he prohibit the brothers to return to their beds to rest on these days once lauds is finished. Rather, he tacitly leaves it to their judgement to return to their beds if time permits, because they have risen earlier because they are worn out by the length of the night's divine service. The things he will not permit to happen, he openly forbids. He makes clear what things he urges to be done. But the things about which he is silent in this way, he leaves to the judgement and discretion of the abbot and the brethren.

13.

Hence, at the end of nocturns, of lauds and of the day hours of the divine service, he makes it clear that after the "Lord have mercy," the Lord's Prayer should be said. He says: "At other services, let the last part of this prayer be said so that all may answer 'But deliver us from evil'" (Mt 6:13; RB 13:14). He does not indicate that a collect prayer should be said there, for after having mentioned "But deliver us from evil," he says: and "thus the night vigils are ended" (RB 9:11). And again: "And it is completed" (RB 12:4; 13:11). And still again: "The dismissal" (RB 17:10). No collect prayer is indicated lest it be tedious for those praying or the preceding Lord's Prayer[54] be said negligently, for one does not find any prayer more precious than the Lord's Prayer through which the divine service is ended. Then, at the end of compline, he adds: "Lord have mercy, a blessing and the dismissal" (RB 17:10). He refers to the blessing which has been used from his time to ours.

14.

He says: "Let us always remember what the Prophet says: 'Serve the Lord with fear' (Ps 2:11); and again: 'Sing wisely' (Ps 46 [47]: 8)" (RB 19.3). By this he wanted it understood that he had shortened the divine service, so that it could be completed zealously, joyfully and without weariness. It is known to be short; and where a section is long, it is sustained by all the breath of all the singers; where it is truly short, it proceeds without the support of such breathing. Wordiness in the divine office counts for almost nothing before God. It is fitting that one standing before a king —blessed Benedict says this (RB 20:1)—address him in an honourable way. Afterwards he adds: "In community, prayer should always be kept short" (RB 20:5). He recommends prayer before each canonical hour. Later he commands: "A kiss of peace should not be offered the guest unless prayer has preceded" (RB 53:5). If almighty God is the one to be greeted, it is all the more proper that a brief prayer precede. Then later when they are taking part in the psalmody, they will not be less attentive to the psalmody because they will not be fatigued by the length, preceding prayer.

15.

Sleeping Arrangements

[RB 22]

"As provided by the abbot, monks receive bedding suitable to their way of life" (RB 22:1). This is clarified when he speaks of the clothing of the brethren: "For bedding a mat, a woollen blanket and a light covering as well as a pillow will be sufficient" (RB 55:15). "Let them sleep clothed" (RB 22:5), that is with the single, simple woollen garment which is worn next to the skin, so they will not lie naked. They do not wear two layers of clothes, because they could not stand it.[55] They sleep "girded with belts or cords" (RB 22:5) so that the clothes they are wearing will not fall off and so that they will not appear naked.

16.
On Punishments
[RB 23–30]

He also says: "If any brother be found stubborn or disobedient or proud" (RB 23). Right after that he adds: "provided he understands the nature of this penalty, let him be subjected to excommunication" (RB 23:4). This is not the lawful excommunication pronounced by priestly right under the stole, but one which by simple words separates from the company of the brothers, in the refectory, or the divine office in choir, or the dormitory, or the like. To those with understanding, this penalty brings greater shame and confusion[56] than corporal punishment. Since corporal punishment is to be inflicted on those who lack such understanding, he adds: "If, however, he lacks understanding, let him undergo corporal punishment" (RB 23:5). In other words, let him be punished with blows or other physical chastisements, because such a one is not led to amendment by words and scarcely by the sharp pains of the flesh.

B. COMMUNITY TASKS AND CARE FOR THOSE WITH SPECIAL NEEDS

17.
The Cellarer
[RB 31]

He speaks this way of the cellarer of the monastery: "He will provide the brothers their allotted amount of food"—that is without any predetermined measure being explicitly established—"without any pride *[typo]* or delay" (RB 31:16). In the word *typo* one should understand *ti,* that is "to you" and *"in*[57] *po,"* that is, power. Hence, the cellarer should not say to himself: "Yours is the power to give and deny when you wish," so he may give more and better food to whom he wishes and may provide less and worse food for whom he wishes. To some extent, people of the world, dispensing allotments in the administration of princes, are wont to do this at time. He is not to arrogate this power. For he does not supply a greater portion to the one who needs than to the one who is not needy, when he gives more to the one who needs than to the one who is not needy.[58] Nor will he delay[59] to give the things which are to be given.

18.
Kitchen Service
[RB 35]

Then there follows: "On Saturday the brother who is completing his work will do the washing" (RB 35:7), washing out stains and dust with branches when this is necessary. Again: "Both the one who is ending his service as well as the one who is about to begin are to wash the feet of everyone" (RB 35:9). This refers to the mandatum. Again: "One hour before mealtime, let him receive something to drink" (RB 35:12=38:10). This means a snack, that is bread and wine, specifically bread dipped in drink, bite sized, so it can be mixed with drink. Afterwards it says: "Let the one going out receive a blessing," that is a prayer. Immediately there follows: "Once he has received the blessing, let him enter;" this refers to a suitable prayer[60] (RB 35:17–18).

19.
Care for the Sick, the Young and the Aged
[RB 36–37]

Then he says: "Moreover, to regain their strength, the very sick and infirm may eat meat" (RB 36:9). He wishes this to be understood to mean the meat of four-footed animals and of birds; it excludes no meat which men ordinarily eat. "But when they have become better, let all abstain from meat as is customary" (RB 36:9). This refers to the meat of four-footed animals, for those who are healthy do not usually eat them and their juices, while those who are sick do. The healthy do eat the flesh of birds because these are clean and they do not induce lusty desire in those who eat them.[61] Then he adds: "and let them anticipate the canonical hours" (RB 37:3). This refers to eating before the hours laid down in the *Rule*. The aged and the children eat their meal earlier than others; they eat and more often than others, and they receive more delicate food.

20.
Table Reading
[RB 38]

Again he says: "And thus after receiving a blessing[63] let him begin his reading" (cf. RB 38:4) with a prayer of blessing. And immediately he adds: "No one should presume to ask there about the reading or about anything else, lest occasion be given [to the devil], unless the superior should wish to say a brief word of edification" (RB 38:89). At that time, he who was the superior of the rest gave salutary admonitions regarding the reading to those present before they parted. They were few then; later, as numbers grew, they avoided this lest on such an occasion they break forth in idle words. "The brother who is reader for the week should receive a drink," as was said above, "before he begins to read, because of the Holy Communion" (RB 38:10). For in the time of blessed Benedict, the one who was going to read, because he uttered holy words, was like one serving at the altar and so he received Communion[64] on Sunday. But[65] then he had lunch so that he would not be fasting when he read and perhaps feel faint. Another factor that the Father [Benedict] wished understood was that after receiving Communion, each believer should keep a more close and careful watch than usual on himself in all things.

21.
The Measure of Food
[RB 39]

He adds: "Two cooked dishes should suffice for all the brothers" (RB 39:3). "Cooked" here refers to those foods which are placed on the fire and moved back and forth with a stick so that they will not be burned. Then he says: "If there is any fruit or fresh vegetable, let a third be added" (RB 39:3). He indicates beans and peas and other vegetables of that kind which are collected fresh from the field, just as fruit is taken from trees; he orders these to be placed before the brothers as a third food, not cooked, but with the shell removed. Fish and cheese and eggs are also included in this third dish; they are a treat. The loving father does not mention these explicitly because he knew that monks would not abstain from them. Hence he neither forbade them nor did he mention them explicitly. Afterwards he writes: "Let everyone, except the very weak and sick, completely abstain from eating the meat of four-footed animals" (RB 39:11). He makes no mention of birds because he did not forbid the healthy to eat them. Since in his time the monastic way of life was crude and still rather unusual, the same father avoided forbidding them the eating of meat completely. He permitted them to make use of birds as food.

C. DISCIPLINES OF THE COMMON LIFE
[RB 43–52]

22.
Making Amendment
[RB 43–46]

Then he says: "So that he may be seen by him and by all, until he does penance by public satisfaction at the end of the work of God" (RB 43:6) by prostrating and asking pardon. And again: "Thus let the guilty one make satisfaction by this" (RB 43:12), that is by prostrating upon the ground. Then he adds: "When the time comes that he wants what he earlier refused, or anything else, let him receive nothing at all, until he makes suitable amendment" (RB 43:19). Because of the disrespect he showed, everything, however necessary, will be denied to the impudent brother until he demonstrates his amendment by humble penance.[66] And again: "Then at the feet of all that they may pray for him" (RB 44:4) to God whom he has offended by his grave faults. And immediately: "Let them keep doing this until he [the abbot] blesses them" (RB 44:10) by greeting them in public and arousing humility. And then: "And if he do not seek satisfaction," that is by seeking pardon with his body flat on the ground, "there he will be humiliated before all. Let him be subject to greater punishment" (RB 45:1) by the punishment of his flesh before all. And when he says: "If the cause of sin is hidden in his soul," he means if a brother has secretly deviated in any matter or has secretly committed[67] some sin. "Let him make it known only to the abbot or to spiritual seniors" (RB 46:5) by confessing the bond of sin and thus gaining forgiveness.

23.
Penitential Practices
[RB 49]

He adds: "Everyone should, however, make known to the abbot what he is offering up since it should be done with his blessing and approval" (RB 49:8). None of the brothers should abstain completely from the regular communal food and drink regularly and communally set before him in the community of his brothers unless he has the permission of his abbot. Nor, when the brothers are gathered for the common prayers and works should he by his own decision depart from them, unless he is allowed to do so by his spiritual father. However, for the sake of his body he can lawfully withdraw part of some of the regular and common food and drink regularly and communally set before him in the community of his brothers. However, he should do this so that clamour does not arise, by regularly and humbly following the common custom of the monastery in all matters without complaint.

24.
Prohibition of Eating Away from the Monastery
[RB 51]

He writes afterwards: "Let him not presume to eat outside, even if someone strongly urges it, unless he should be commanded to do so by his abbot" (RB 51:1). If he does otherwise, let him be excommunicated with that excommunication by which an insolent and disobedient brother is separated from the communion and company of his brothers until he makes satisfaction, as was said above.

25.
Reverence
[RB 52]

And he says:[68] "When the work of God is finished, let all go out with the greatest silence; and let a reverence be made to God" (RB 52:2). Let them bow reverently as they go out, and let them have reverence in their other works which are done in the service of God, and not rush into anything wanton or excessive.

D. HOSPITALITY
[RB 53]

26.

Then he says: "When a guest is announced, let the superior or the brethren hurry to meet him with the courtesy of charity, and first let them pray together" (RB 53:3). All are led to church in order to offer adoration. Thus, the brothers pray to God so that they will not violate their order with the guests; the guests, that they will be better for seeing their way of life. And again: "With their heads bowed or their whole body on the ground, they adore Christ in the guests, just as He is received in them" (RB 53:7). For it is as though Christ is present when guests arrive and they receive them, or when guests depart and they bless them as they go, or they bow before the guests out of reverence for Christ or ask pardon from them (cf. RB 5:6). He adds immediately: "And after this let all courtesy be shown him" (RB 53:9). This includes both friendly and companionable conversation and every bodily need. And further: "Let the abbot pour water for the guests' hands" as a duty[69] of humility "and let both the abbot and the community wash the feet of all guests" (RB 53:12–13). The latter means those for whom the abbot enjoins such a service. For when the guests whom blessed father Benedict received were about to eat, he gave them water for their hands; and when they had risen from table, he washed their feet. He did this because of the example offered at the Last Supper to the disciples by the Son of God. Women's feet he did not touch; but he modeled contempt of the world for them both in his dress and in his holy way of life. At that time monks did not yet feel the press of a tumult of strangers crowding upon them. However, those who did come to them were seeking there nothing else but Christ; and they found Him there in the holy works.

E. CLOTHING

[RB 55]

27.

Outer Clothing

Then he proceeds: "The clothing given the brethren should vary according to the local conditions where they live and the climate" (RB 55:1). He shows here that clothing is given to the brethren with regard to what they can stand and so that they may not murmur. Where the area is so cold that necessity forces men to not forego the use of warm clothing, both linings of lamb's wool and tunics with a lamb's skin collar are monks' clothing which meets with the heavenly Judge's approval, because they make a superfluity of clothes unnecessary. Then there follows immediately: "We believe that for each monk a cowl and a tunic will suffice in temperate regions" (RB 55:4). The cowl should be full and extend to the ankle; it should have short sleeves so that the hands extend slightly beyond them. It should have two openings running down below the armpit on each side. The capuch was attached above. It is a special sign of the monk when he has it on his head, signifying he looks neither left nor right toward the world. There should be a wool tunic somewhat less ample than the cuculla, but wider in the legs and reaching to the feet. The sleeves should not be too wide or too tight and should reach to the hands. There should be an opening going down on each side below the armpit. The tunic[70] had no capuch.

28.
Underclothing

Then he adds: "Let the abbot take care of the measurements, so that they will not be too short" (RB 55:8) as some lay people's are. Rather, let the monks' clothing reach to the ankle, because they do not wear underclothing in their quarters. Hence, he adds: "Brothers going on a journey should get underclothing from the wardrobe, and when they return they should wash it and give it back (RB 55:13). From this one can understand that monks who lived under the teaching of this father did not use underclothing except when they were leaving their quarters. The majority of people did not use underclothes at that time so, because of the customs of the people and as a sign of childlike simplicity and humility, the same father did not allow underclothes to his disciples while they were in their[71] quarters. But he granted them to those who were going out on horse or on foot[72] as an example of chastity and for the sake of manly decency and human respect. But now in our times, because the customs of men indicate it, it is not displeasing to God if monks, because of the blasphemy of sacrilege which they might experience in naked flesh, wear underclothes so that they will not be naked and touch flesh with flesh, and thus be reminded of fleshly sins.

29.
Bedding

He continues: "For bedding monks need a mat, a blanket" (RB 55:15). The latter is made of coarse cloth or from hemp and shaped like a sack, filled with some sort of bedding material and placed upon the mat which the monks had spread over their bed. [In the same sentence] he says they should have a "light covering" of wool, which is spread over the bed during the day for decorum and with which they may cover themselves at night when they wish. Immediately he says:

"Let all the things that are necessary be provided by the abbot" (RB 55:18). He mentions a cincture which is cinched over the tunic so it will not slip off because they sleep without underclothes; and a "garter" which was worn next to the skin from which the tied sandals hung; a "handkerchief" or cloth made of line with which they wiped away their sweat while they were working.

F. The Reception of Brethren
[RB 58–62]

30.
Children
[RB 59]

Later he says: "And with the offering let them wrap the petition and the hand of the boy in the altar cloth" (RB 59:2). This means that the petition of the parents of a body is committed to writing as confirming evidence when they offer him to God, just as that of the one who himself promised stability, conversion and obedience before God and His saints in his own consecration as described earlier.

31.
Priests
[RB 60]

Then he writes: "If any of the order of priests asks to be received into the monastery, do not let consent be granted too quickly" (RB 60:1). Such a priest is understood to be one who presided over a charge or a deanery or a parish and so could, with difficulty, force himself[73] into subjection. There is no question of a bishop, because it would not be fitting that one who was a ruler of people's souls and was the master of an abbot, should be subject to an abbot. If a bishop wishes to convert, he should do it only by penance, without submitting to any teaching authority. Then he says: "If there is question of an appointment or another matter in the monastery" (RB 60:7)—referring to responsibilities and teaching[74] offices or external business matters which are to be handled with consultation—"let him keep the place which is his according to entry into the monastery" (RB 60:7): "the place," that is his profession of their way of life of humility and subjection which gains for him a good and high grade (1 Tm 3:13). Let him keep before the eyes of his heart what place he is going to enter since he received the monastic habit in the monastery which shows contempt for the world, "not that which is granted him out of reverence for his priesthood" (RB 60:8). This means he is not to pay attention to the place of teacher that earlier was his when he was a teacher and master among the people and clergy. Let him not think or judge himself more prudent or learned or more ready or circumspect in speech than his brothers who were raised in the cloister, nor that because he dwelt in the world and consorted with seculars he surpassed them all. Instead, because of his voluntary conversion by which he freely subjected himself to the discipline of the *Rule* and out of reverence for his priesthood, he will give good example with the others and will show himself obedient and subject in all matters.

32.
Monks from Elsewhere
[RB 61]

And the same father then says: "If afterwards he wishes to pledge his stability, such a wish is not to be denied." And then: "Not only should he be joined to the community if he asks to be received. He should even be urged to stay so that others may learn from his example, for the Lord is served in every place and one fights for the same king" (RB 61:8–9). This father first wrote that "the novice is to be received in the oratory where he should promise his stability before all" (RB 58:17); and then he added: "He states his promise in a petition in the name of the saints whose relics are there" (RB 58:19); and then he says this: "Such a wish is not to be denied" and "Indeed, let him be urged to stay" and, again, "Because the one Lord is served in every place" (RB 61:8–9). He wishes this to be understood as follows. On account of his own instability, a monk secretly or wantonly leaves his monastery in which he has promised stability and made his petition as is written above. He comes to a distant region and there sees a monastery of his type of religious life. He is moved by repentance to want to stay there in stability. He has asked for confirmation that he may be received. In such a case, if he is worthy, even if because of his lengthy travels he does not and could not have letters of commendation, it will be better that he be received than that entry be denied him. For if he were not received, he might be discouraged by weakness, infirmity, old age, or some other hindrance, or by the length of the return journey to the monastery he left, and in despair he might return to the world. Then, remaining in the world, he would perish in soul and body. However, it would be much better for him if he could somehow return to his monastery which he left without the permission of his spiritual father or seek forgiveness, than if he stubbornly remained in the other[75] monastery. Especially is this the case if he knows that the discipline of the monastic life is observed there in his former monastery. The father affirms this in what follows: "Let the abbot beware of ever granting membership to a monk from another known monastery without the consent of his abbot or a letter of commendation" (RB 61:13). He does not wish that monks obliged by their stability and petition move from place to place as they choose without permission. Rather they are to keep their vow with firm tenacity.

G. Relations among Members of the Community
[RB 62–73]

33.
Priests
RB 62]

There follows: "Let him not, because of his priesthood, forget the obedience and discipline of the *Rule*, but let him advance more and more toward God. Let him always keep that place which is his by entry into[76] the monastery, except in his duties at the altar" (RB 62:4). This means that a priest monk who is ordained in his monastery should not become proud because of his priesthood but, with loving devotion, keep before the eyes of his heart that place of humility and subjection for which, following the example of Christ (1 Cor 2:1), he received the monastic habit and embraced contempt of the world. At that moment he subjected himself to the service of God and man. Above all, let him think humbly that he became the servant and minister of God when he yoked himself to the service of the altar. In this way he will show himself more humble and more obedient in all things. He will recall that he humbly and devoutly received the habit of a monk because of which he will, without pretence, think himself worthy and obedient in everything. But he must also recall that because of the way he subjected himself to God in the duties of the altar (1 Cor 4:1), he will sincerely account himself humble, meek and in last place (Mt 11:29).

34.
Respect for Seniors
[RB 63]

Then he adds: "Whenever the brothers meet each other, the junior should ask a blessing from the senior" (RB 63:15), that is by way of the greeting, he will show himself to be subject to his senior in all humility.

35.
Prayer for Absent Brethren
[RB 67]

Then he says: "All those who are absent should always be commemorated at the closing prayer of the work of God" (RB 67:2). This last[77] prayer of the work of God is the Lord's prayer for, as was said above, the work of God is ended with this prayer since he showed that the litany, the Lord's prayer and the dismissal, occur there. When the disciples of this blessed[78] father pray in the same prayer "But deliver us from evil," they add regarding those absent: "and your servants and our absent brothers," thereby commemorating them.[79] They did not have fully developed collect prayers at that time and so they often ended the divine service with the Our Father.

36.
Boys
[RB 70]

Then he says: "Boys up to the age of fifteen should, however, be carefully disciplined and supervised by everyone" (RB 70:4). That is, just as a boy under fifteen years of age is delicate of body, so he is delicate of mind. For the time being he has no fear and can be bent toward what is good; he does not dare wantonly to resist those who correct him. But when he reaches fifteen years he is already in the bloom of youth. Like a flowering tree strengthened by the pith and fluids in it, so the powers of his mind surge up so that he disdains to accept and bear the childish corrections he used to accept.

37.
Straight to the Goal
[RB 72]

Finally the blessed father affirms all these things: The kingdom of heaven will lie open to those who do these things (cf. RB 72:11). All the things which are described in this *Rule* are not too slack[80] nor too restrictive; they look to the right and not81 to the left, so that they lead the one who keeps them straight to heaven.

38.
Conclusion

Therefore I, a poor little female in form, heard these words from Wisdom who taught me the obscure things in the *Rule* of blessed father Benedict so that I could present them openly. So let the meek, mild and timorous hear them, let them understand them[82] with a loving heart, and let them accept them with humble devotion.

COMMENTARY ON THE REQUEST OF THE CONVENT OF HUNNIENSIS

1.

The whole community writes. Later in paragraph 4 of their petition (PE 4), they complain about the arbitrariness of their prelates. Perhaps this suggests a collegiate church of canons, subject to a diocesan bishop who is not a member of the community.

Hildegard is a temple of the Spirit and a spouse of Christ beloved of God, two titles which were applicable to any Christian but which seem especially appropriate to a visionary (temple of the Spirit) and an abbess (mistress) who is renowned for her sanctity (spouse of Christ, beloved of God). She is revered; hence the petitioners address their request to her.

2.

The attributes of sanctity and spiritual vision are repeated: they rejoice in her holiness and they have already delighted in the revelations of her thought. It is clear, therefore, that Hildegard is already an established figure since she was already known to them.

3.

The first sentence of this paragraph is enigmatic. "Order" could refer to a way of life governed by a *Rule* (e.g. Cluniac, Victorine) or even to a community. The petitioners' order is honoured by Hildegard, "although we are quite different from you in all respects." Here they refer to "the Rule of our blessed father Benedict"; in PE 4 they mention "our blessed father Augustine." The most likely meaning is that they consider themselves followers of St. Augustine, whose Order Hildegard has held in honour, but they also have great respect for Benedict and so can also refer to him as their father.

The petitionary letters reads "omnes in commune" (all of us together); the RB favours the equivalent forms "omnes pariter" (20:5; 49.3)[83] and "pariter" (together: 53:4; 72:12). They ask for a "memorial" (memoriale vestrum); remembering and forgetting are key concepts in Hildegard's writings.[84]

4.

"Perjurers" (perjuri) is the one word in the first sentence of this paragraph which suggests the gender of the petitioners. There may be one or two issues at stake here: the petitioners may be indicating that they themselves are unjustly accused of violating the synodal decrees, whereas their prelates do indeed violate the canons and the rule, or they may be saying their prelates force them to live in such a way that they are rightly accused of being violators of the rule. The first interpretation seems more likely.

The main fault of the prelates, from the petitioners' point of view, is that they arbitrarily impose added ("servile") burdens which go beyond the rule.[85] They want a rule governed by the laws of the church and the *Rule.* Their prelates are "sarabaites" (RB 19). *The Rule of Augustine* is very short and does not impose many minute regulations.

5.

Like Peter de Celle, a Benedictine who wrote his School of the Cloister[86] for a canon regular, the petitioners recognise the close affinity of all claustrals.

The petitioners end where they began with a request for counsel and prayer from one who is wise and holy and conclude with a final salute to Hildegard's maternal love (cf. PE1–2). They ask her to pray that they may have a share in the Spirit who guides her.

COMMENTARY ON HILDEGARD'S EXPLANATION OF THE RULE OF BENEDICT

1.

Hildegard often begins her works with a passage deprecating her human capacities as an unlettered woman.[87] Such avowals of incompetence are common in twelfth-century authors. Hildegard, however, adds a different twist. Since there is no human source for her teaching, she can then claim divine enlightenment and warrant. Viewed another way, Hildegard, as a woman who was not highly educated, could not hope to receive a hearing unless she claimed supernatural authority.[88] In this instance she invokes not just the "true light" but also "the memory of Blessed Benedict," thereby echoing the petitioners' PE3. Hildegard's claim to being uneducated and therefore taught by the Holy Spirit is supported by the fact that apart from the Bible and, in this work, *The Rule of Benedict,* she does not quote earlier or contemporary Christian authorities. Although she was certainly influenced by Christian tradition, her vocabulary and ideas are often freshly minted.[89]

Hildegard mentions the grace and power of the Holy Spirit three times in this one brief paragraph. She will mention them often in subsequent paragraphs.

Hildegard says that she has been enlightened regarding the more difficult and obscure matters in the *Rule*. Like Hildegard herself, St. Benedict was filled with the grace of the Holy Spirit. Although the virtues she attributes to St. Benedict are quite general, they seem to reflect the influence of Book 2 of the *Dialogues* of Gregory the Great which, with the *Rule,* provide almost all the information we have about Benedict. The devil looms large in Gregory's life of Benedict (Dial. 2:2, 2:8, 2:10, 2:16, 2:20, 2:25, 2:30);[90] Gregory's description of Benedict's mystic vision was universally known (2:35; cf. 2:16, 3–8: Benedict was one spirit with God); Gregory shows that Benedict had the virtues of all the just (2:8–9);[91] Benedict had the gift of prophecy from the Holy Spirit (2:21, 3–4).

2.

Gregory says that Benedict's *Rule* was "outstanding for its discretion" (2:26: regulam discretione praecipuam). *The Rule of Benedict* insists on discretion in the abbot; Gregory says abbot Benedict could not have lived other than he legislated (2:36); Benedict's discretion is one of the most insistent themes of Hildegard's commentary. By insisting on Benedict's discretion, Hildegard is implicitly justifying her own interpretation of the *Rule,* which is marked by discretion instead of an inflexible commitment to literal observance or austerity.[92] Hildegard is also implying an affinity between Benedict's discretion and her own conviction that physical and spiritual health are based on harmony.[93]

The circle or wheel is a recurring symbol in Hildegard's works, which often stands for the creative dynamism of the divine nature.[94] Here the metaphor seems to be of a barrel of wine or beer lying on its side, in which a spigot has been placed at a convenient height.[95] The idea of drinking wisdom or grace occurs in Prov 8:35, 12:2, 18:22, Is. 12:3 and is a theme of Jn 4. The metaphor is continued in the first line of Ex3.

Moses is a favourite figure of Hildegard;[96] he also appears in this work (Ex4).

3–4.

Once again, Benedict is endowed with all the virtues of the just. Benedict's doctrine was perfected in the Holy Spirit; hence it ought not to be altered. The opening words of the RB echo the didactic tone of the wisdom tradition,[97] and thus identify the author as a divinely guided teacher.

5.

Hildegard jumps from the "pius pater" of RB, Prol. 1 to Chapter 1 on the kinds of monks on which she gives some rather general comments and emphasises the importance of stability. The nail fixed in the centre of the circle of Ex3 suggests stability as well as discretion.

6.

Having already passed over the doctrinal content of the prologue, Hildegard now fails to comment on important chapters: (2) on the abbot; (3) calling the community for counsel; (4) instruments of good works; and (5) obedience. She treats silence at length as a practical matter: evidently it was an issue in cloisters of her day. Her position is that Benedict allowed speaking times when they were necessary but did not establish a certain time each day for speaking. This was a matter he left to the judgement of the abbot. Speaking should be in common and moderate. Here Hildegard is referring to immoderate silence, not to the disciple-master relationship or to evil speaking, two topics that loom large in RB. It must be noted that she makes no mention of sign-language.

7.

In her lengthy discussion of the arrangement of the divine office, one of Hildegard's concerns is to decide whether what RB says of one hour applies to other hours: usually she says it does not.

Just as Christ was a healer, so too did Benedict have the touch of a physician; his discretion kept him fixed and stable at a healthy point of balance in matters such as silence and speaking. His rule for sleeping and keeping awake shows the same healthy balance.[98]

Hildegard shares the common mediæval view that habits of eating—like the times of sleep when food is digested—correlate with inclinations towards sexual arousal.

Benedict used the words "pietas" and "pius" (e.g. in the phrase "loving father") only in the prologue. In the same way Hildegard uses it at the end of this paragraph.

8.

Benedict's *Rule* is also moderate in requiring the monks to stay awake after Vigils and Lauds.

9.

Commenting on RB 9–12 (On the Night Office), Hildegard simply says that no "Our Father" should be added where Benedict does not provide for one.

10.

This paragraph deals with which of the short readings at the Divine Office should be memorised and recited by heart. Like modern commentators on the RB, Hildegard interprets Benedict's provisions for reading and meditation (48.13,23; 58.5) as including memorisation of texts.[98] As usual Hildegard sees a practical justification for this legislation.

11.

Hildegard emphasises hearing and listening to the word of God. She picks out for particular emphasis the Gospel passage: "Behold we have left everything and followed you" (Mt 19:27). In so doing, she applies a passage specifically to monastics which exegetes traditionally applied to the Apostles or to all believers and which the liturgy has used as the Communion antiphon for the Common of a confessor who was not a bishop.[99]

The implication of the last part of the paragraph seems to be that Hildegard considered daily celebration of the

Eucharist usual, but foresaw that there were exceptions.[100] In the *Scivias* (2.6.46, ed. Führkötter, p. 270), she says that Communion should be received under both species except by those who are likely to spill the wine.

12.

Hildegard here discusses one sentence in RB, Ch. 12 which deals with Vigils on Sunday. Offering the unlikely interpretation that on Sundays there might be an interval between Vigils and Lauds, she concludes that members of the community could go back to bed during this time. She bases this reading on what, for her, is a key principle for her interpretation of the *Rule:* the fact that Benedict is quite clear about those things he wishes to be done and openly forbids what he does not wish to happen. He leaves those things which he does not mention to the discretion of the abbot and the members of the community.

13.

Here and in Ex35, Hildegard maintains that Benedict did not end the hours of the Office with Collect prayers but that all the hours, with the exception of Compline, conclude with the Lord's Prayer.

14.

Hildegard enunciates the principle that liturgical participation should be "zealous, joyful and without weariness" (in gaudio et sine taedio studiose). With this principle in mind, she says that St. Benedict shortened the divine service101 and that wordiness has no place in liturgical prayer (cf.Mt 6:7). She thus applies to liturgical prayer as a whole what Benedict may have intended to apply only to the silent prayer or to the Collect prayer following the Psalms.[102]

When Hildegard says that long sections (distinctiones) should be sustained by the breath ("ad spiritum"), she is perhaps referring to the practice of taking deep breaths at the start of a section and then breathing at different times during it. She may also be referring to the Holy Spirit.

Hildegard's suggestion that a brief prayer should precede each canonical hour combines two disparate ideas of St. Benedict. This may be a criticism of the rather lengthy accretions which preceded the Office in mediæval monastic practice.

15.

Hildegard interprets RB 22.5 in the light of her argument in Ex28 that it was fitting in her time that monastics wear underclothes. Here she says that they should take off their outer clothes and sleep in their underwear if it became too warm. Her concern that monastics not be seen naked is repeated in Ex28.

16.

Hildegard comments on the penal code of the *Rule* in one brief paragraph. She points out that monastic excommunication is something quite different from formal ecclesiastical excommunication.[103] She herself was to experience some of the complications of the latter sort of excommunication near the end of her life.[104]

17.

Hildegard's commentary on the work of the cellarer is carefully constructed. He is to supply (1) the allotted portion (2) without favouritism and (3) without delay. To give more to one who needs more does not imply that the cellarer is either exceeding the allotted portion or showing favouritism. *Tuphos* (pride, vanity) is a term used frequently by Greek Christian writers and it is occasionally found in Augustine.[105] Although her etymology of the word is false[106]—the root meaning of the word is "smoke"—she has captured the meaning of the word very well: *tuphos* is the opposite of humility.

Hildegard conflates the provisions for a snack before meals for readers (RB 38) and kitchen servers (RB 35) which was to be provided in order that the servers be strengthened for their work. In allowing a reader a drink[107] before the midday meal, Benedict also seems to have wanted the reader to rinse out his mouth lest he spit out any of the Eucharistic wine while he was reading out loud. Hildegard does not here advert to this (see Ex20), but seems to equate mistum=prandium [midday meal]=bread and drink [panem et potum]=bread dipped in drink [panem potui intinctum]=bite-sized pieces [offae] which make it possible for bread to be mixed with wine. It is possible that she meant prandium [midday meal] to be in apposition with hora refectionis [mealtime], and the rest in apposition to mistum.

19.

Hildegard interprets Benedict's references to meat in the light of RB 39.11 where he forbids the healthy to eat the meat of four-footed animals (carnium quadrupedum: see Ex21). She believes that red meat is more likely to nourish sexual inclinations than the meat of fowl.[108]

20.

Hildegard implies that the custom of superiors commenting on the table reading had lapsed by her time.

Returning to the drink given to the table reader because of Communion (see Ex18), Hildegard interprets this to mean that since he has fasted before Communion, he will need to eat so that he will have the strength to do his reading: a feat which, before the days of microphones, required considerable exertion.

The parallel which Hildegard draws between reading holy words and serving at the altar is reminiscent of the parallel which Benedict makes between the tools of the monastery and the vessels of the altar (RB 31.10). Although her statement that

Benedict wanted those who had received Communion to keep a more careful watch on themselves is interesting, its connection with the context is obscure. Perhaps her point is that Communion should put one in a proper frame of mind for the reading of holy words.

In her last sentence, Hildegard seems to imply that only those who served at the altar regularly received Communion on Sundays.

21.

Hildegard is expansive in her interpretation of RB 39. To the two cooked vegetable dishes and a third dish of fruit and fresh vegetables, she adds fish, cheese and eggs. In this she invokes her principle of leaving to the discretion of Benedict's followers what he does not forbid or command. She does, however, seem to consider Benedict's endorsement of the eating of the meat of fowls (see Ex19) as a concession which might no longer be needed.

22.

Here Hildegard conflates two sections of RB 44. He who has been excommunicated from oratory and table for serious faults is to prostrate himself at the abbot's feet and "then at the feet of all that they may pray for him" (RB 44.4). Those, however, who have been excommunicated only from table for less serious faults "are to make satisfaction in the oratory . . . until he [the abbot] blesses and says 'Enough'" (RB 44.9–10). It is not clear on grammatical grounds to whom Hildegard is referring in the clause "by greeting in public and eliciting humility" It could either be the abbot or the penitent himself.

Hildegard abridges into three principles the prescriptions of the *Rule* for making amendment: (1) those who transgress against the *Rule*, the abbot or the community, should make public satisfaction; (2) such of these who will not make public satisfaction should receive public corporal punishment; (3)

those who commit a secret fault should confess it only to their superior or to their spiritual seniors. She does not distinguish here between monastic and sacramental confession.[109]

23.

Here, as in *Scivias* 1.6.82, Hildegard passes from a discussion of confession to alms and corporal punishment as means to make satisfaction (ed. Führkötter, p. 88). Her emphasis here, however, is that one should abstain from food only with the permission of the abbot and within the context of the common life. She enunciates three guidelines: (1) unless the abbot permits it, voluntary abstinence should not include all the food and drink at a meal; 2) one should not be absent from other common works and prayers without the abbot's permission; 3) partial abstinence at meals is allowed for the sake of one's health, provided that it is done unobtrusively. Hildegard concludes that, in general, one ought to follow the common custom of the monastery regularly, humbly and without complaining. The fact that she leaves room for personal discretion in matters of food and drink for the sake of bodily health is indicative of the high value she placed on physical health.

24.

Hildegard omits the first phrase of Benedict's short chapter and adds a description of excommunication.

25.

Here Hildegard sees reverence as an attitude towards God which should accompany all the works done in God's service[110] and unruliness as its opposite.[111]

26.

Reverence, then, should be shown guests. After the guests have been greeted promptly, they are taken to the church where the monks pray that their hospitality will not violate their daily routine (ordo) and the guests pray that they will be edified by the monks' way of life (conversatio).

Hildegard emphasises Benedict's point that Christ is served in the guests. The courtesy (humanitas) extended to them includes conversation, care for their bodily needs and the washing of their hands and feet (mandatum: see Ex18). Benedict, she says, was able to devote more time to guests than a modern superior could since there were fewer guests in his day and, furthermore, they were more religiously motivated.

Throughout this paragraph, Hildegard emphasises the effect of good example. The abbot washes the feet of the guests because of Christ's example. The guests are to be edified by the example of the daily routine and works of the monks. Although Benedict did not touch the feet of women, he did give them an example by his dress[112] and demeanour. Here and in Ex31 Hildegard sees outward deportment in the context of "contempt of the world" as a sign or example for others.[113]

27.

In the matter of clothing, discretion must take into account the climate and situation, and Hildegard prefers that monks try to get by with few but suitable clothes. Her descriptions of the cuts of the garments are somewhat obscure. Her edifying interpretation of the capuche is repeated in her Letter 51 in response to the prior of Eberbach[114] where she also discusses the significance of the cuculla.[115]

28.

Here Hildegard gives two reasons for her views on the wearing of underwear: custom and decorum. Underwear was not in common use in Benedict's day but he recommended that, for decorum's sake, it be worn outside. By Hildegard's time, however, it was customarily worn and thus she legislates its use both inside and outside the monastery, especially since, she says, its use may lessen carnal temptation. In Ex15 she had said that contemporary monastics should sleep in their underwear.

29.

Hildegard had discussed bedding in Ex15, but since Benedict brings up again the topic here, so does Hildegard. Her interpretations of the items of clothing and bedding mentioned by Benedict are interesting and reasonable, if occasionally questionable. The bed, mat, blanket and a light covering specified are similar to present-day sleeping equipment for a mountain cabin: bunk, pad, sleeping bag and dust cover.

30.

The parents of child oblates are to put their petitions in writing, like adult novices. Hildegard concludes the paragraph by saying "as described earlier." This is a clear reference to the provisions of Chapter 58 of the *Rule* on the procedure for receiving candidates, a chapter upon which, in fact, she has not commented.

31.

Hildegard gives a detailed commentary on the reception of priests. As a ruler of souls, a bishop was not to be received into a monastery since it would be inappropriate for such a one to be subject to an abbot. In the same way, Hildegard considers it unwise to receive priests who are used to positions of authority. If admitted, they should esteem their present humble and subject position as more valuable than their priestly rank. His status as priest should oblige him to be an example of obedience and subjection in his freely chosen position as monk. Finally, he should beware lest he think himself wiser than those who were raised in the monastery since their childhood. Here Hildegard seems anxious to obviate tension between oblati/nutriti on the one hand, and conversi on the other, a realisation perhaps based on her experience as an oblata, a sister, and an abbess.

32.

Acceptance into a monastery of persons who had been professed in other monasteries was an abrasive topic in the twelfth century.[116] In Ex5, Hildegard indicated the importance of stability and she closes this paragraph by insisting on the obligation of monks to remain faithful to this vow: they should not move to another place without permission. She narrows the issue down to the specific situation of a monk who, through his own lack of stability, leaves his original monastery without authorisation.[117] Her imagined renegade travels far and wide and, finding a monastery similar to his own, is moved by repentance and asks to be allowed to join it. Although, abstractly speaking, it would be better for such a one to return to his original monastery, there remains the possibility that he might die before he is able to return to the community he abandoned. Thus, in Hildegard's judgement, it is better to receive him into the new monastery even if he has no letters of recommendation. She reiterates Benedict's caution that admittance should never be given to a monk from another known monastery without consent of his previous abbot.

33.

In this paragraph, Hildegard returns to the question of the place of priests in the monastery. Her concern, however, is no longer about priests who have exercised administrative and teaching authority but, rather, any priest. She develops the idea broached in Ex31 that the priest-monk should find in his monastic profession and in his priesthood a motivation to humility and obedience, since both commit him to a life of service to God and others. Here, as in Ex31, the considerable attention Hildegard gives to the position of priests in the monastery may well reflect a concern at the community at Hunniensis.

34.

When a junior greets his senior by asking a blessing, he signifies his subjection to him in humility.

35.

In Ex13 Hildegard did not think that in Benedict's time the hours of the Office ended with a collect prayer. Here she concludes that the commemoration of the absent brethren which Benedict had mandated for the end of Compline was attached to the Our Father.

36.

In this paragraph, Hildegard elaborates on a single line of the *Rule* regarding the disciplining of boys up to the age of fifteen.[118]

37.

In this passage, which is an inclusion with Ex2, Hildegard returns to Benedict's discretion. Where there she said that Benedict aimed neither too high nor too low, here she says that he deviated neither to the right nor to the left.

38.

Hildegard's concluding paragraph is an inclusion with Ex 1: she is a poor woman taught by Wisdom itself. She ends with a word of encouragement to others who, like her and the fearful community of Hunniensis are not among the mighty of this world and who therefore are able to hear, understand and accept these words with loving heart and humble devotion.

END NOTES

1. The two most accessible accounts of Hildegard's life and works are Sabina Flanagan, *Hildegard of Bingen (1098–1179): A Visionary Life* (New York: Routledge, 1989) and Barbara Newman, *Sister of Wisdom* (Berkeley: University of California Press, 1987). The rapidly expanding literature on Hildegard is monitored by Werner Lauter, *Hildegard-Bibliographie: Wegweiser zur Hildegard-Literatur and Hildegard-Bibliographie,* V. 2: 1970–1982 (Alzey: Der Rheinhessischen Druckwerkstätte, 1970, 1984). For literature published after 1984, see Gertrud Jaron Lewis, *Bibliographie deutschen Frauenmystik des Mittelalters,* Bibliographien zur deutschen Literatur des Mittelalters 10 (Berlin: Erich Schmidt Verlag, 1989): pp. 66–145.

2. Marianna Schrader, *Die Herkunft der heiligen Hildegard,* Quellen und Abhandlungen zur mittelrheinische Kirchengeschichte 43 (Mainz: Gesellschaft für mittelrheinische Kirchengeschichte, 1981).

3. Franz Haug, "Hildegardis und Richarda" *Studien und Mitteilungen zur Geschichte des Benediktinerordens* 47 (1929): 597–601; Flanagan, 180–184.

4. For this sketch of Hildegard's life I rely primarily upon Flanagan, pp. 1–40. Also helpful is Adelgundis Führkötter. "Hildegard von Bingen: Leben und Werk" in *Hildegard von Bingen, 1179–1979,* ed. Anton Brück (Mainz: Gesellschaft für mittelrheinische Kirchengeschichte, 1979): pp. 31–54. Peter Dronke's chapter on Hildegard in his *Women Writers of the Middle Ages* (New York: Cambridge University Press, 1984) is instructive for many features of Hildegard's life and personality. For Hildegard's works, see Marianna Schrader and Adelgundis Führkötter, *Die Echtheit des Schrifttums der heiligen Hildegard von Bingen* (Köln: Böhlau, 1956).

5. Erika Opelt-Stoevesandt, "Zum Bild der heiligen Hildegard von Bingen" in *Inter Confessiones: Beiträge zur Förderung des interkonfessionellen und Interreligiösen Gesprächs,* ed. Anne Marie Heiler, Marburger theologische Studien 10 (Marburg: Elwert, 1972): pp. 34–39. Flanagan (pp. 193–213) presents theories regarding the nature of Hildegard's illness.

6. Wolfgang Seibrich, "Geschichte des Klosters Disibodenberg" in *Hildegard von Bingen, 1179–1979,* p. 55; Heinrich Büttner, "Studien zur Geschichte von Disibodenberg" *Studien und Mitteillungen des Benediktinerordens* 52 (1934): 1–46.

7. *Scivas,* ed. A. Führkötter and A. Carlevaris, Corpus Christianorum, Continuatio Medievalis, vol. 43, 43A (Turnhout: Brepols, 1978). See *Hildegard of Bingen: Scivias,* translated by Mother Columba Hart and Jane Bishop, Classics of Western Spirituality (New York: Paulist Press, 1990). A translation of parts of the *Scivias* is included in Francesca Maria Steele [Barley Dale], *The Life and Visions of St. Hildegard* (St. Louis: Herder, 1915). Much of this work is translated into English by Bruce Hozeski, *Scivias* (Santa Fe: Bear and Co., 1986). There is a complete German translation by Maura Böckeler, *Wisse die Wege* (Salzburg: Otto Müller, 1981). See Frater Henri Boelaars osb, *Commentaar op de Miniaturen in Scivias van Hildegardis van Bingen* (Doetinchem: Sint Willibrordsabdij, 1984) and Matthew Fox, *Illuminations of Hildegard of Bingen* (Santa Fe: Bear and Co., 1985).

8. Hildegard von Bingen, *Lieder,* ed. Pudentiana Barth, M. Immaculata Ritscher and Joseph Schmidt-Görg (Salzburg: Otto Müller, 1969); *Der heiligen Hildegard von Bingen, Reigen der Tugenden: Ordo Virtutum; Ein Singspiel,* ed. Audrey Ekdahl Davidson (Kalamazoo: Medieval Institute, 1984). See Peter Dronke, *Poetic Individuality in the Middle Ages* (New York: Oxford University Press, 1970); Maura Böckeler, "Aufbau und Grunddanke des Ordo Virtutum der h. Hildegard" *Benediktinische Monatschrift* 5 (1923): 300–310; "Beziehungen des Ordo Virtutum her hl. Hildegard zu ihrem Hauptwerke Scivias" *Benediktinische*

Monatschrift 7 (1925): 25–44, 135–145. Eight of Hildegard's songs, translated by Kent Kraft, were published in *Vox Benedictina* 1/3 (1984): 157–161 and 1/4 (1984): 257–263.

9. *Liber simplicis medicinæ [=Physica]* (PL 1117–1352); *Liber compositae medicinæ [=Causae et Curae]*, ed. P. Kaiser (Leipzig: Teubner, 1903). These works are well served by German translations: *Hildegard von Bingen, Naturkunde*, tr. Peter Riethe (Salzburg: Otto Müller, 1980); *Heilskunde: Das Buch von den Grund und Wesen und der Heilung der Krankheiten*, tr. Heinrich Schipperges (Salzburg: Otto Müller, 1981); *Das Buch von den Steinen*, tr. Peter Riethe (Salzburg: Otto Müller, 1979). See Irmgard Müller, *Die pflanzlichen Heilsmittel bei Hildegard von Bingen* (Salzburg: Otto Müller, 1982) and Wighard Strehlow and Gottfried Hertzska, *Hildegard of Bingen's Medicine* (Santa Fe: Bear and Co., 1987).

10. Hildegard's letters have been recently edited: *Hildegardis Bingensis Epistolarium*, ed. L. van Acker, Corpus Christianorum, Continuatio Mediævalis 91–91A (Turnhout: Brepols, 1991, 1993). Previously they were available only in PL 197, cols. 145–382 and J. B. Pitra, *Analecta spicilegio solesmensiparata: sanctæ Hildegardis opera* (Monte Cassino, 1982): pp. 328–582. Some of the letters have been translated into German by Ludwig Clarus [pseud.], (Regensberg: C. J. Mainz, 1954) and by Adelgundis Führkötter, (Salzburg: Otto Müller, 1965). Two letters written by Hildegard and Elisabeth of Schönau have been translated by Kathryn Kerby-Fulton and Dyan Elliott, "Self-Image and the Visionary Role in Two Letters from the Correspondence of Elisabeth of Schönau and Hildegard of Bingen" *Vox Benedictina* 2/3 1985): 204–223 and reprinted in *On Pilgrimage: The Best of Ten Years of Vox Benedictina* (Toronto: Peregrina Publishing Co.), pp. 535–547.

11. Ed. Pitra, *Analecta*, 1–244; German translation, *Den Mensch in der Verantwortung: Das Buch der Lebensverdienste*, tr. Heinrich Schipperges (Salzburg: Otto Müller, 1972).

12. PL 197, cols. 739–1038. A partial English translation is available in Matthew Fox, ed. *Book of Divine Works, With Letters*

and Songs (Santa Fe: Bear and Co., 1987). Heinrich Schipperges has translated the work into German: *Welt und Mensch: Das Buch De Operatione Dei* (Salzburg: Otto Müller, 1965). The work is discussed by Adelgundis Führkötter, "Die Gotteswerk" *Benediktinische Monatschrift* 29 (1953): 195–204, 306–314.

13. Maria Laetitia Brede, "De Klöster der heiligen Hildegard Rupertsberg und Eibingen" in *Hildegard von Bingen, 1179–1797*, pp. 77–94.

14. The early *vita* by Godfrey and Theodoric is in PL 197, cols. 91–130 and has been translated into German by Adelgundis Führkötter: *Das Leben der heiligen Hildegard* (Salzburg: Otto Müller, 1980). The *Acta inquisitionis* from the thirteenth-century canonisation process are edited by P. Bruder in *Analecta Bollandiana* 2 (1883): 118–129. Guibert of Gembloux's vita was edited by Pitra in *Analecta*, pp. 407–415.

15. Much of Guibert's correspondence with and about Hildegard is published by Pitra, *Analecta*, pp. 328–404. For a summary of Guibert's life and connections with Hildegard, see Marianna Schrader, "Wibert von Gembloux: Schicksal eines Mönches im 12. Jahrhundert" *Erbe und Auftrag* 37 (1961): 381–392.

16. One of the few places in Hildegard's work where Benedict is mentioned occurs in *Scivias*, ed. Führkötter, 2.5.20 (pp. 193, 724) which name, in an odd lapse, Hozeski translates as John the Baptist (pp. 111–112). Near the end of Ep. 2 to Pope Eugene III (PL 179, col. 150C), Hildegard avows that "Father, in accord with the words of your blessing and according to the Rule of St. Benedict, I remain with my sisters in the cloister of the place shown to me by heaven . . . ."

17. Other information may be obtained from her letters to monastic correspondents: see Flanagan, pp. 161–164.

18. Ed. Pitra, pp. 7–8, no. 1.

19. For references, see Carolyn Walker Bynum, *Jesus as Mother* (Berkeley: University of California Press, 1982): p. 32 and *Docere Verbo et Exemplo*, Harvard Theological Studies 31 (Missoula MT:

Scholars Press, 1979): pp. 104, 113 n. 39, 148. J. P. Schmelzeis, *Das Leben und Wirken der heiligen Hildegardis* (Freiburg im Breisgau: Herder, 1879), p. 291, refuses to commit himself on the suggestion that Hunniensis was Hüningen in Alsace. Johannes May, *Die heilige Hildegard von Bingen* (Kempten: Kösel, 1911): p. 447, opts for the "Hunsrückkloster Ravengiersburg." The case for Ravengiersburg is summarised by M. Pot in an unpublished thesis at the University of Leiden (1987), pp. xxvi–ixl. I wish to thank Fr. Henri Boelaars osb of St. Willibrordsabdij, Slangenburg, for sending me a copy of this thesis.

20. Ferdinand Pauly, Springiersbach, *Trierer theologische Studien* 13 (Trier: Paulinus, 1962): pp. 16–58; Consuetudines Canonicorum Regularium Springirsbacenses-Rodenses, ed. Stephanus Weinfurter, Corpus Christianorum, Continuatio Medievalis 48 (Turnhout: Brepols, 1978).

21. Pitra, 8:495.

22. Thus M. Pot, p. lxix, following Schrader, *Echtheit*, 160n.

23. My thanks to Bibliotheksoberrat Dr. Podehl for supplying a printout of the text in Wiesbaden, Hessische Landesbibliothek, MS 2, fols. 421ra–425rb.

24. Wiesbaden, Hessische Landesbibliothek MS 2, the so-called Riesenkodex (=W) and Migne's Patrologia Latina (=M) both read: s(ancto) Roberto in Pingis.

25. M: paradisici; W. paradysiaci.

26. W: vobis; M: nobis.

27. W: provoluti; M: convoluti.

28. W: praedictaeque; M: praedictae.

29. This clause is singular ("quisque ... despicit"), but the next one is plural ("ipsi sibi sunt lex").

30. W: aggravemur; M: aggravamur.

31. M: Qui quamvis; W: Quae quamvis.

32. W: legalibus; M: regalibus.

33. W. necessaria satageritis; M: necessariae sategeritis.

34. W: Sed; M: Si.

35. W: De regula sancti Benedicti Hil[degardis].

36. W: Lucidissima dona; M: Lucidissima.

37. W: ita quod mens ipsius in amore Dei ardebat et in virtutibus ut aurora rutilabat; Pitra (=P): ita quod mens ipsius in amore Dei ardebat, et quod in virtutibus ut aurora rutilabat; M: ita quod mens ipsius in amore Dei rutilabat.

38. P, W: inbecillus sive infirmus sit; M: imbecillis sit.

39. W: O fili; M; fili.

40. W: ut; omitted by M.

41. W, P: loquendi concedatur licentia; M: loquendi gravitatem licentia.

42. W, P: quae oportet; M: quae opus.

43. W: loquendi; M omits.

44. W: fere; M omits.

45. W: surgent; M: surgunt.

46. M: cum; W omits.

47. W: vertens; M: vertunt.

48. W: incurret; M: incurreret.

49. W: sentiet; M: sentiret.

50. W: meditationi; M: meditationibus.

51. W: cum necessitas se immerserit; M: cum necessitas se emerserit.

52. W: intendit; M: intendi.

53. W: haberi; M omits.

54. M: oratio; W: oratione.

55. W: possent; M: possunt.

56. M: confusionis ruborem; W: confusionis ruboris.

57. W: in; M omits.

58. W, P: quod non plus indigenti quam non indigenti annonae subministret; M: quod non plus indigenti annonae subminstret.

59. W: faciet; M: facit.

60. M: oratione; W: orationi.

61. W: manducabant; W: manducabunt.

62. W: accepta benedictione; M: omits.

63. M: communicabat; W: communicabant.

64. W: Sed; M omits.

65. M: poenitendo humiliatus; W: poenitendo humilitatis.

66. W: commisit; M: permisit.

67. W: dicit; M: dixit.

68. W: officium; M: exhibitionem.

69. W: tunica; M omits.

70. W: sua; M omits.

71. M: sive equestribus sive pedestribus; W: sive in equis sive pedes.

72. W: animum suum; M: animam suam.

73. P, W: interiorum; M: magisteriorum.

74. W: alieno; M: alio.

75. W: in; M: omits.

76. W: oratio ultima operis; M: oratio ultimi operis.

77. W: beati; M omits.

78. P notes an addition in the margin of a manuscript: In hoc commemorationem absentium facientes. Cum autem redissent, in eadem oratione dominica illis reversis dicebant: 'Sed libera nos a malo' et famulos tuos fratres nostros de via revertentes. Amen.

79. P, W: nec nimis remissa, nec nimis constricta; M: nec nimis constricta.

80. W: non; M omits.

81. W: ea; M omits.

82. It also uses "pariter" alone (53:4; 72:12) and expressions with "communis," but not "omnes in commune."

83. See Christel Meier, "Vergessen, Erinnern, Gedächtnis im Gott-Mensch-Bezug" in *Verbum et Signum* [Festschrift F.Ohly], ed. Hans Fromm et al. (Munich: Fink, 1975): 1: 156–187.

84. Whether this is to be taken to refer to manual work is not clear. Hildegard does not comment on RB 48, and so passes up a chance to discuss monastic work. She does not write about work very often, but it is possible to develop some elements of a theology of work from her writings. See H. Boelaars, "Hildegardis

en de Arbeid" *Benedictijns Tijdschrift* 20 (1959): 83-91.

85. Peter of Celle, *Selected Works,* tr. Hugh Feiss (Kalamazoo: Cistercian Publications, 1987): pp. 14-15, 28-29, 63-130. Cf. Bynum, *Docere.*

86. *Scivias,* prol., 1,1, ed Führkötter and Carlevaris, p. 3, lines 9–11; p. 8, lines 41–43; *Liber divinorum operum* prol. (PL 197, col. 7411AB);. Ep. 77, ed. Pitra, *Analecta* 8:539; Ep. 51 (PL 197, col. 260B).

87. Barbara Newman, "Hildegard of Bingen: Visions and Validation" *Church History* 54 (1985): 163–175. Her final comment—"To account for the exceptional claims of a woman like Hildegard, we need to consider both the dynamics of mystical illumination and its refraction through the cultural and psychological prism of gender"—could serve as the thesis for Flanagan's study. See also Newman, *Sister,* pp. 34–41; Bernhard Gertz, "Tönend vom lebendigen Licht: Hildegard von Bingen und das Problem der Prophetie in der Kirche" *Erbe und Auftrag* 49 (1973): 171–189; Friedhelm Jürgensmeier, "St. Hildegard 'Prophetissa Teutonica'" in *Hildegard von Bingen, 1179–1979,* pp. 273–293.

88. Führkötter, introduction to her edition of the *Scivias,* pp. xiv–xviii.

89. See Adalbert de Vogüé's comments in the introductory volume to his edition of the *Dialogues,* Source Chrétiennes 251 (Paris: Cerf, 1978): pp. 100–103.

90. de Vogüé, pp. 135–138. *Dialogues* 2.8.8 declares: vir iste spiritu iustorum omnium plenus fuit. This phrase was used in the fifth antiphon for Lauds in the monastic office for the Feast of St. Benedict (March 21): Vir Domini Benedictus omnium justorum spiritu plenus fuit.

91. Hildegard, *Heilkunde,* ed. Schipperges, pp. 275–290.

92. Ruth M. Walker-Moskop, "Health and Cosmic Continuity: Hildegard of Bingen's Unique Concerns" *Mystics Quarterly* 11 (1985): 19–25.

93. E.g., *Liber div. op.* 2.1–18 (PL 197, cols. 751–764); Scivias, ed. Führkötter, 1.3.1–6 (pp. 40–44). See Hans Liebeschütz, *Das allegörische Weltbild der heiligen Hildegard von Bingen,* Studien der Bibliothek Warburg 16 (Leipzig: Teubner, 1930): pp. 23, 107 n. 2, 122.

94. Generally Hildegard recommended drinking wine or beer, rather than water. If water is to be taken, it should be boiled first: *Heilkunde,* ed. Schipperges, pp. 191–192.

95. See Pitra's index, *Analecta* 8:612; *Scivias,* ed. Führkötter, p. 808.

96. See *RB 1980: The Rule of Benedict,* ed. Timothy Fry (Collegeville: Liturgical Press, 1981): pp. 145–147, 156–157.

97. Hildegard, *Heilkunde,* ed. Schipperges, pp. 152–161, 276–278; see Heinrich Schipperges, *Die Benediktiner in der Medizin des frühen Mittelalters,* Erfurter theologische Schriften 7 (Leipzig: St. Benno, 1964): pp. 20–22, 48–54.

98. RB 1980, p. 250 n. 446 (with extensive citations from the literature).

99. *Bibliorum sacrorum cum glossa ordinaria . . . et postilla Nicholai* 5 (Venice, 1603): 323–324; *Graduale sacrosanctæ romanæ ecclesiæ* (Paris; Desclée, 1952).

100. For Hildegard's Eucharistic theology, see Willibrord Lampen, "Sint-Hildegard en de h. Eucharistie" *Benedictijns Tijdschrift* 20 (1959): 92–100; Ep. 47 (PL 197, col. 22BC); Gerhard Müller, "Schau des Geheimnisses: Die Eucharistie in der prophetischen Theologie Hildegards von Bingen" *Internationale katholische Zeitschrift Communio* 8 (1979): 530–542. Hildegard speaks ill of those who are too ill to receive the Eucharist for fear of vomiting it up. She describes a ceremony of "spiritual communion" for these people in which the elements are placed on the sick person's head and heart while an appropriate prayer is said.

101. For a comparison of Benedict's Office with that of his predecessors, see RB 1980, pp. 379–414.

102. RB 1980, pp. 412–413. On Hildegard's prayer, see Adelgundis Führkötter, "Wie Hildegard von Bingen betete" *Geist und*

Leben 52 (1979): 324–335.

103. See RB 1980, pp. 420–426.

104. Flanagan, pp. 184–190.

105. *Confessions* 3.3.6; 7.9.13, ed. Verheijen, CCSL 27 (Turnhout: Brepols, 1981): p. 29, line 17; p. 101, line 5. Ep. 22.6, ed. Goldbacher, CSEL 34 (Vienna: Tempsky, 1895): p. 59, line 5.

106. Although wrong, this etymology has a distinguished history. See Gregory the Great *In Euangelia Homiliæ* 43, 2 (PL 76): quod agitur typo superbiae. Most Christian writers of the later Middle Ages used Isidore as the basis for their interpretation of this word: Typhus vero, quae se ab aqua inflat. Vnde etiam ambitiosorum et sibi placentum ominum tumor typhus dicitur (*Etymologiae* 17.9. 101, ed. W. M. Lindsay [Oxford: Oxford University Press, 1957).

107. RB 1980, pp. 237, 411. Mistum or mixtum: diluted wine or a drink in which bits of bread are mixed. In his note to RB 38.10 E. Manning opts for the former interpretation: *Règle de Saint Benoît,* tr. H. Rochais (Paris: Desclée de Brouwer, 1980): p. 106, while Georg Holzherr thinks it meant diluted wine: *Die Benediktsregel* (Zurich: Benziger, 1982): p. 213.

108. Cf. Ex7. Cassian believes there is a close connection between eating and sexual desire, but does not single out meat: *Conférences* 22.3, ed. E. Pichéry, Sources chrétiennes 64 (Paris: Cerf, 1959): pp. 116–119. In his edition of the *Rule,* A. de Vogüé discusses abstinence from meat in early monasticism: *La Règle de Saint Benoît,* Sources chrétiennes 186 (Paris: Cerf, 1971): pp. 6, 1103–1107. H. Musurillo gives further references in his "The Problem of Ascetical Fasting in the Greek Patristic Writers" *Traditio* 12 (1956): 1–64.

109. In *Scivias* 2.6.82, 84–87 (Führkötter, pp. 295–297), Hildegard speaks eloquently of confessing one's sins to a priest or to others or even to the elements if a priest is not available. Elsewhere she speaks of confession with reference to the responsibility of clergy in binding and loosing (*ibid.* 2.6.93–100, pp. 300–304).

110. See the entries for reverentia in the index to *Scivias,* ed. Führkötter, p. 847.

111. In *Liber vitæ meritorum* 5.2.3, ed Pitra, pp. 184–185, reverentia opposes scurrrilitas.

112. See Ex31 for the translation of habitus as clothing or habit.

113. See *Scivias* 3.10.13 and 26, ed. Führkötter, pp.560, 567–568; *Liber vitæ meritorum* 4.14, ed. Pitra, pp. 153–154; "Song in Honour of St. Ursula and Companions:" *Carmina* 65, ed. Pietra, p. 456. The song in honour of St. Ursula has been translated by Peter Dronke in "Hildegard of Bingen as Poetess and Dramatist" in *Poetic Individuality* (Oxford: Clarendon Press, 1970): pp. 161–163; by Barbara Newman in *Sister of Wisdom: St. Hildegard's Theology of the Feminine* (Berkeley: University of California Press, 1987): pp. 225–226; and by Kent Kraft in "Hildegard of Bingen: Three Songs" *Vox Benedictina* 1/3 (1984): 160–161.

114. Ep. 51 (Ad griseos monachos), PL 197, cols. 262B–263A.

115. See A. Steiger, "Was sagt uns St. Hildegard über unsere Kukulle?" *Cistercienser-Chronik* 41 (1929): 211–231.

116. St. Bernard's defence in this matter is outlined in his *On Precept and Dispensation* (Treatises I, Cistercian Fathers series 1 (Shannon: Irish University Press, 1970): pp. 138–144.

117. By thus narrowing the issue, Hildegard avoids some difficult questions: e.g., whether monks may transfer to a stricter monastery in order to keep the *Rule* more faithfully.

118. Compare *Scivias* 3.3.6, ed. Führkötter, p. 379, lines 290–298; *Liber divinorum operum* 1.4.78 (PL 197, col. 860B).